Illustrator:
Cheri Macoubrie Wilson

Editorial Project Manager:
Charles Payne, M.A., M.F.A.

Editor:
Janet Hale, M.S. Ed.

Editor in Chief:
Sharon Coan, M.S. Ed.

Art Director:
Elayne Roberts

Art Coordination Assistant:
Cheri Macoubrie Wilson

Cover Artist:
Marc Kazlauskas

Product Manager:
Phil Garcia

Imaging:
Ralph Olmedo, Jr.

Acknowledgements:
ClarisWorks software is ©
1991–1996 Claris Corporation. All
Rights Reserved. *ClarisWorks* is a
trademark of Claris Corporation,
registered in the U.S. and other
countries.
Kid Pix 2® and *Print Shop*® are
Copyright Brøderbund Software,
Inc. 1998. All Rights Reserved.

Publishers:
Rachelle Cracchiolo, M.S. Ed.
Mary Dupuy Smith, M.S. Ed.

TECHNOLOGY CONNECTIONS

FOR

Weather

PRIMARY

Author:

Jennifer Overend Prior, M.S. Ed.

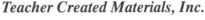

Teacher Created Materials, Inc.

6421 Industry Way

Westminster, CA 92683

ISBN-1-57690-397-4

©1999 Teacher Created Materials, Inc.   Made in U.S.A.

Teacher Created Materials

Table of Contents

Teacher Created Materials Computer Integration: An Introduction

Using This Book

Technology Connections for Weather was created with you in mind. Perhaps you are an avid user of computer programs and related technology. Possibly you are somewhat proficient in the ways of technology and wish to get to know how to use a computer more effectively, but you lack the time or know-how to even get started. Or maybe you are one of many in this technologically advanced society who still shies away from computers altogether; you have no knowledge of computers, and the idea of using computers with your students scares you half out of your wits! Whoever you are, this book is for you. From the most proficient to the least knowledgeable, you can now integrate the use of computers and related technology with your students into your everyday curriculum.

Most of us are probably somewhere in the middle as far as computer literacy is concerned. We may type here and there at home or at school. We may use computers with our students in the most popular way, playing games. We want to teach our students the myriad of purposeful applications computers have to offer, but this takes time (which we all know teachers have little enough of already), and we may lack the most rudimentary knowledge: where to begin. In addition, teaching computer literacy in itself without purpose or long-range objectives seems a waste of time. What we need is the ideal situation—ideas to teach computer skills by integrating meaningful computer activities into our existing curriculum. This book will do that for us.

This book offers integrated computer projects your students can complete. They are meant to complement topics about Weather that you may already teach your students; they are not units in and of themselves. **The activities are designed to be used with various word processing, painting, and desktop-publishing programs you may use in your school, specifically *ClarisWorks* (word processing), *Kid Pix* (painting), and *Print Shop Deluxe* (desktop publishing). Many software companies are now publishing numerous comparable programs which may act as substitutes for the former. If your school doesn't have *ClarisWorks*, for example, you can still implement the activities with an alternative word processing program such as *WordPerfect*.**

All you need to know to help your students successfully complete the computer projects described in this book is how to access a program, open files saved to disk, and click and drag the mouse.

Refer to the program basics sections to familiarize yourself with the programs you may not feel comfortable using. When you see words that are **bolded**, that means to click on those directional cues. Some directions have two **bold...words** connected by three dots. You should click on the first direction, drag down, and release the mouse on the second. So the direction **File...Save** means to click on "File," drag down to "Save," and then release.

The time necessary to complete these projects adjusts to your schedule. Your students may complete them in one hour or one week, depending on the availability of computer usage, your students' knowledge of the programs you use, and the length of the project.

Read through the activities to decide which ones are right for you. Then hop on that computer and type away.

Computer Integration: An Introduction (cont.)

Technology All Around Us

Computers and computer-related technology have steadfastly become an integral part of our everyday lives. As consumers, a great portion of our purchases is made using technology.

We find it at the grocery store, the gas station, restaurants, etc. It's in hotels, laundromats, and car washes. Challenge yourself to live one day—or even half a day—without the use of advanced technology. You may think you can hide out at the beach and let one day in the age of technology pass you by. But consider your means of travel to and from the beach. Most of today's cars have computer chips monitoring their internal systems. If you consider riding your bike, think of the manner in which it was designed and marketed prior to its purchase. Walking? Civil engineers may have had a technological hand in designing the roads, sidewalks, or sewer systems upon which you tread. And what of the beach itself? Scientists are continually monitoring wave motions, tidal patterns, beach erosion, current weather trends, and sea life—all with the use of advanced technology.

Technology has also infiltrated our school systems. Payroll, food services, budget and finance, as well as other areas within a school or district, have begun to depend on computers to perform tasks and manage large amounts of information. Student records no longer take weeks to process. If a teacher feels specific information about a child is required immediately, he or she can simply request a fax of the necessary documents.

And what of the classroom itself? Computer and technology usage may vary from school to school, but chances are they all use some technological applications in some form or other. Your school may be one to use video technology to broadcast a live (or taped) morning show throughout the school. You may take advantage of multimedia programs such as the *Magic School Bus* CD-ROM series (see Bibliography, page 48).

Yes, computers and computer-related technology are all around us. It is here now while our students are still young. It will be here when our students graduate and become productive members of society. And it will be here when our students' grandchildren are faced with their own set of technological advances. Things are moving so fast now, we can hardly keep up with the changes ourselves. A computer bought today may be archaic within the year. Regardless of the changes taking place now, we must still take the time to prepare our students for the world of technology they will encounter in their futures. The following pages and subsequent activities will answer the question of what we can do today to help our students learn for tomorrow.

4

Computer Integration: An Introduction *(cont.)*

Looking Ahead

Our jobs as educators have evolved to encompass a great quantity of subject matter. We are still required to teach the basics of yesterday yet are expected to also provide our students with the training and skills they will need to carry them through tomorrow's technological advancements. Computers are the tools to pave the way for our students' futures. With the use of computers, we can teach the skills students need to learn, model the role of technology in our society, and provide experiences necessary for their successes in life.

Few people would disagree that computer experiences are necessary in our schools so that our future leaders will be prepared to realize their dreams, regardless of the career choices they may decide upon for themselves. But more important than general computer knowledge is working computer knowledge. We, as educators, should be providing real-life experiences with today's advanced technology. But, more importantly, we should not lose sight of the ultimate goal: communication. Through the use of computers, we can open up a whole new world of communication for our students.

Many of us realize the important role computers will play in our students' futures. We also realize that we have a responsibility to our students to prepare them to utilize computers as learning tools and as an effective way of communicating with others. Nearly every school across the country uses computers in some way or other to help teach students basic learning skills, as well as word processing skills. The beauty of today's technology is that we can integrate skills learning with technology-related activities. Together, you and your students will use the power of computers to create astounding projects. Have fun!

Welcome to the Age of Technology!

With the use of computers, educators can . . .

- ◆ teach both academic and computer literacy skills
- ◆ model the role of technology
- ◆ provide real-life learning experiences
- ◆ teach students to communicate effectively

Integrated Applications Software:
An Introduction

Most computer users are familiar with basic word processing applications. Word processing allows the typist much more freedom when creating a document. It used to be that when mistakes were made on a typewriter, the typist needed to start over. Not so with the help of today's technology. Word processing allows the writers to delete, add, change, style, and format their work, all with the touch of a few keys.

And if typing were not enough, many programs such as *ClarisWorks*, *Microsoft Works*, *WordPerfect*, etc., also include drawing, painting, database, and spreadsheet applications. This allows the user a variety of opportunities to enhance what was once just a typewritten piece of paper.

ClarisWorks is a common integrated software program that utilizes word processing, drawing, painting, spreadsheet, database, and communications applications. This seemingly simple program can accomplish quite complicated word processing tasks if you know how to use the applications. Refer to "*ClarisWorks* Basics" to learn how to effectively use the basic applications *ClarisWorks* has to offer. Additional applications are described in the activities when they are called for. If you are generally familiar with this program or are using an alternative word processing program, take a look at the activities that accompany *Technology Connections for Weather* in "Integrated Applications Software Activities."

ClarisWorks Basics

This is a brief guide through the word processing application of *ClarisWorks*. Refer to this section if you need assistance when implementing any of the *ClarisWorks* activities.

Word Processing

Upon opening the *ClarisWorks* folder, choose **Word Processing** and click **OK**. You will begin working on a new document. Type as you would on a typewriter. When you come to the end of a line, the computer will automatically return to the next line. Only use the return (enter) key on the keyboard when you want to start a new paragraph.

Task Bar Basics

You can select the line spacing, document layout, and alignment from the task bar that is displayed below the ruler. Clicking the **Body** box to the far right will allow you to choose other word processing options such as bullets, checklists, etc.

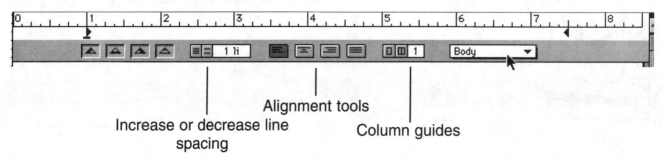

Increase or decrease line spacing

Alignment tools

Column guides

Integrated Applications Software: An Introduction *(cont.)*

ClarisWorks **Basics** *(cont.)*

Text Options

- You can change the type of letters you wish to use before you begin typing by clicking on **Font** and dragging to the type of letters you like.

- Clicking and dragging on **Size** will adjust the size of letters in your document.

- One final text option to consider is the style of letters (italics, bold, etc.). Click and drag **Style** to view the options available.

Spell Checker

If you wish to check your document spelling, click **Edit** and drag down to **Writing Tools...Check Document Spelling**. If the computer does not recognize a word in your document, it will offer alternatives. You can select one of the alternatives listed and click **Replace**. Or you can type the word you need in the box marked "Word:." If the word is correct but not in the computer database, choose **Skip** to tell the computer to overlook this word.

Editing

Chances are that once you have finished typing, you will wish to make some changes. The cursor is your way of communicating with the computer. You can move the cursor, using the arrow keys to the text area you wish to change, or you can use the mouse to move the cursor to the appropriate place on the page and then click.

To edit text, move the cursor in front of the text you wish to edit. Clicking and dragging the text you wish to change will highlight it. Any changes you make will only be applied to this part of the text. This is useful if you wish to make headlines in a larger print or a different font and/or style.

To remove text, you can highlight it by clicking and dragging over it and then pressing the delete key. Or you can click the cursor in front of the text you wish to remove and press the delete key to erase the text one character at a time.

Quitting

Be sure to save your document before you quit. Go to **File... Save**. Choose the appropriate file in which you wish to place your document (either on the hard drive or on a disk). Then type in a name for this particular item. Click **Save**. The computer will save your document for you. Then you can **File...Quit** the program. When you wish to work on your document again, go to **File...Open**. Choose the file and click **Open** once again.

Activity 1: Temperature Log, Graph, and Reflection

Teacher Note: This project has been created using *ClarisWorks*. Any word processing and spreadsheet program can be used, if properly modified.

Students record daily high temperatures, create a graph to represent the information, and write a reflection of the activity in *ClarisWorks*.

Background Knowledge: reading a thermometer

Step 1: Log of Weekly High Temperatures

Review the use of and how to read a thermometer to determine daily temperatures. Discuss temperatures that are considered to be hot and cold in your area and in other locations in the country. Ask students to determine when would be the best time of day to record the high temperature.

Have students keep track of local, daily high temperatures for one week by completing the log on page 11. The information on the log will be used later to create a graph of the week's high temperatures. (See page 32 of the Thematic Unit: *Weather,* TCM 273, by Teacher Created Materials for more temperature activities.)

Step 2: Create a Spreadsheet

Perform the following procedures to create a spreadsheet of the week's high temperatures.

1. Click to open *ClarisWorks*. Then open the **File** menu and drag to **New** to open a new document. Select **Spreadsheet** and click **OK**.

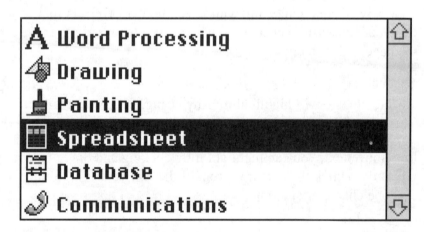

2. Input the data into the spreadsheet cells. To do this, type a different day of the week (Monday–Friday) in the first cell of columns A through E. Below each heading, numerically list that day's high temperature.

8

Activity 1: Temperature Log, Graph, and Reflection *(cont.)*

Create a Spreadsheet *(cont.)*

	A	B	C	D	E
Temp. Template (SS)					
	× ✓				
1	Monday	Tuesday	Wednesday	Thursday	Friday
2	76	72	74	69	71

3. **File…Save** this spreadsheet.

Step 3: Create a Graph

Create a graph of the information from the spreadsheet using the following steps.

1. Click and drag to highlight the data on the spreadsheet.

2. Still in the spreadsheet file, click on **Options** and drag to **Make Chart**. A screen will appear, showing several different kinds of graphs. Click the desired type of graph to represent the data. A bar graph or a line graph are the best choices for this project.

3. The completed graph will have a legend box labeled Series 1, unless modifications are made. To remove legend box, select **Labels** and click on the **X**.

4. A title can also be created for the graph at this point, such as "Daily Temperatures." Click **OK** and the graph will appear over the spreadsheet.

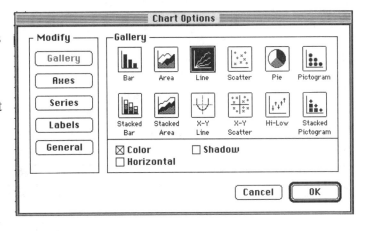

Step 4: Import the Graph into Word Processing

You can easily import the graph of high temperatures from the spreadsheet file to a word processing document.

Activity 1: Temperature Log, Graph, and Reflection *(cont.)*

Import the Graph into Word Processing *(cont.)*

1. In order to import the graph, the image must be highlighted. The graph is highlighted if a dark square can be seen at each corner. If the dark squares are not present, click within the graph area one time. Go to the **Edit** menu and drag down to **Copy**. This will make a copy of the graph so it can be pasted onto a word processing document.

2. Go to **File** and drag to **New** to open a new document. Select **Word Processing** and then click **OK**.

3. From the **Edit** menu, drag to **Paste** and the graph will appear at the top of the page. To change the size of the graph, click once on the image, then click on the dark square in the lower right corner and drag to create the desired size.

Step 5: Writing a Reflection

Have each child tell about his graph and explain what it indicates about the week's temperatures.

1. Click in the area below the graph or press the **Return** key to reveal the cursor.

2. Type a few sentences telling about the graph and the information indicated on it.

3. When the reflection is complete, **File…Save** the document.

Step 6: Finish and Print

Make any desired changes before printing the document. If the graph should be accidentally deleted, immediately select **Undo** from the **Edit** menu and the graph will reappear. **File…Print** the document and display student work on a bulletin board entitled, "Let's Talk Temperature!"

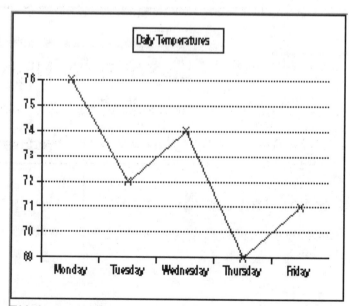

Activity 1: Temperature Log, Graph, and Reflection *(cont.)*

Teacher Note: Copy and cut apart the temperature logs below. Then distribute one to each student for recording local high temperatures each day for one school week.

Name: _____

Log of Daily High Temperatures

Check the high temperature each day. Write the temperatures in the boxes below.

Monday	Tuesday	Wednesday	Thursday	Friday

Name: _____

Log of Daily High Temperatures

Check the high temperature each day. Write the temperatures in the boxes below.

Monday	Tuesday	Wednesday	Thursday	Friday

Activity 2: Weather Newsletter

Teacher Note: This project has been created using *ClarisWorks*. Any word processing/stationery program can be used, if properly modified.

Students keep track of the weather and create a newsletter complete with graphics in *ClarisWorks*.

Background Knowledge: types of weather, interesting weather facts, recognition of weather changes

Step 1: Teacher-Created Newsletter Template

Designing a newsletter involves several procedures. In order to simplify this project for students, follow the directions below to create a newsletter template that can be used by students in writing their own newsletters.

1. Select **File…New** to open a new document in *ClarisWorks*.

2. From the resulting screen, click the box to **Use Assistant or Stationery**.

3. Select **Newsletter** and click **OK**.

4. The Newsletter Assistant will appear. Follow the series of steps on the screen to create the desired newsletter. (You will be asked to click **Next** after each choice made in creating the newsletter.)

5. Click **Create** to assemble the newsletter template. After a brief pause, the newsletter will be created and a screen of Tips & Hints will appear. You may choose to read or print the tips. After doing this, **File…Close** the Tips & Hints window.

6. To remove the crossed lines on the graphics box, select **New View** from the **View** menu. Move the point of the arrow/cursor to touch one of the crossed lines in the graphics square on the newsletter. This will highlight the line (a dark square will appear at each end of the line). Then click **Delete** on the keyboard to remove it. Repeat this process to remove the remaining line.

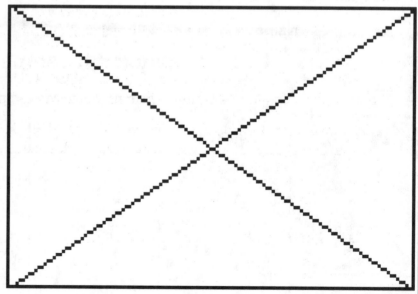

Activity 2: Weather Newsletter *(cont.)*

Teacher-Created Newsletter Template *(cont.)*

7. Now, **File...Save** the document as a template and have students use this outline to create their own newsletters.

Step 2: Ideas for the Newsletter

Generate discussion among your students about what might be included in their newsletters. Ideas could include monthly temperatures in your area, kinds of weather, weather changes, or interesting weather facts discovered in class research (see page 29 of the Thematic Unit: *Weather* by Teacher Created Materials, TCM 273, for a page of weather facts). Have each student write two or three short weather articles to be included in his newsletter.

Step 3: Writing the Newsletter

Open the newsletter template and **File...Save As** the child's name. Type a headline for each article in the chosen location. Then type each article beneath its headline. Adjust the size of the type by highlighting the text (click and drag over the text); then go to **Size** and drag to the desired point size. Adjust the style of the text such as boldface type, italics, etc., by clicking and dragging to highlight the text and selecting from the **Style** menu.

Step 4: Adding Graphics

ClarisWorks provides a library of graphics that can be used in this project to add visual appeal.

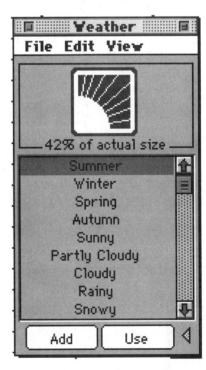

1. The box on the newsletter is the perfect place to add weather graphics. To do this, go to the **File** menu and drag to **Library**; then drag to **Weather**.

2. A small menu of weather graphics will appear. Select the desired picture and click **Use**. The picture will appear on the newsletter.

3. Click on the picture and drag it to the graphics box. The size can easily be adjusted by clicking and dragging the dark square in the lower right corner of the graphic.

Activity 2: Weather Newsletter *(cont.)*

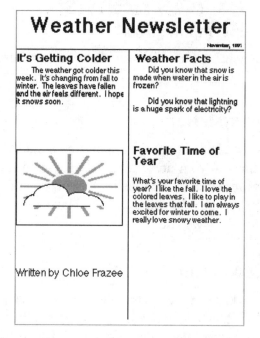

Step 5: Save and Print

Using the **File** menu, drag to **Save** the newsletter. If printing only one of the pages of the newsletter, go to the **File** menu and select **Print**. Then, in the print window, type **From: 1 To: 1**. Have each child choose an article to share with his classmates.

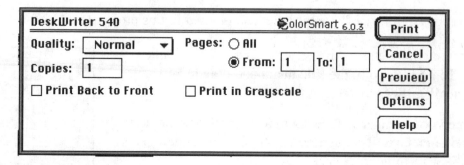

Step 6: Delightful Display

Create an eye-catching display to showcase your students' work.

Trace each child's body onto bulletin-board paper. Have the child cut out his outline and color it in the appropriate attire for his preferred season. Then staple the outline to a wall with the newsletter attached to the hand as shown. Entitle the display "Noteworthy News."

Activity 3: Weather Pie Graph and Reflection

Teacher Note: This project has been created using *ClarisWorks*. Any word processing and spreadsheet program can be used, if properly modified.

Students tally weather conditions for one month, create a pie graph displaying the results, and write a reflection of the activity in *ClarisWorks*.

Background Knowledge: characteristics of different types of weather

Step 1: Group Discussion

Ask students to name different kinds of weather and record their responses on chart paper. Explain that they will be making tally marks on the chart to indicate each day's weather. If desired, provide a copy of the tally chart on page 18 for each student. Then choose a time each day for students to make the proper tallies on their charts. At the end of the month, have students count and record the total for each weather condition.

Step 2: Create a Spreadsheet

Transfer collected data to a spreadsheet by following the directions below.

1. Click to open *ClarisWorks*. Then open the **File** menu and drag to **New** to open a new document. Select **Spreadsheet** and click **OK**.

Sunny Days	Rainy Days
Cloudy Days	**Snowy Days**

Tally Totals:

Sunny Days_____   Rainy Days_____   Cloudy Days_____   Snowy Days_____

Pie graph template (SS

		A	B	C	D	E
		×	✓			
1		Sunny	Rainy	Snowy	Cloudy	
2		15	6	2	7	
3						
4						

Activity 3: Weather Pie Graph and Reflection *(cont.)*

Create a Spreadsheet *(cont.)*

2. Input the data from the tally chart into the spreadsheet cells. To do this, type a different weather condition in the first cell of each column. Below each heading, numerically list the number of days recorded on the tally chart.

3. **File...Save** the spreadsheet document.

Step 3: Create a Pie Graph

ClarisWorks provides several types of graphs for displaying information. The directions below explain how to create a pie graph from the spreadsheet.

1. Click and drag to highlight the data on the spreadsheet.

2. Open the **Options** menu and drag to **Make Chart**. Select the pie graph.

3. While still in the Chart Options screen, add a title to the graph by clicking on **Labels**. Type a title for the graph such as "Weather in November" in the space indicated. When finished, click **OK** and the graph will appear over the spreadsheet.

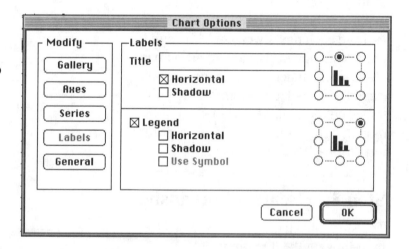

Step 4: Import the Graph into Word Processing

Now that you have a pie graph, you can easily import the graph from the spreadsheet file to a word processing document.

1. In order to import the pie graph, the image must be highlighted. The graph is highlighted if a dark square can be seen at each corner. If the dark squares are not present, click on the graph area one time. Go to the **Edit** menu and drag down to **Copy**. This will copy the graph so that it can be pasted onto a word processing document.

Activity 3: Weather Pie Graph and Reflection *(cont.)*

Import the Graph into Word Processing *(cont.)*

2. Still in the spreadsheet file, open the **File** menu and drag to **New** to open a new document. Select **Word Processing** and then click **OK**.

3. From the edit menu, select **Paste** and the graph will appear at the top of the page. To change the size of the graph, click once on the image, then click on the dark square in the lower right corner and drag to create the desired size.

Step 5: Writing a Reflection

Write a reflection below the graph explaining what each of the pie segments represents. To do this, click in the area below the graph or press the **Return** key to reveal the cursor. Type the reflection and then **File...Save** the document.

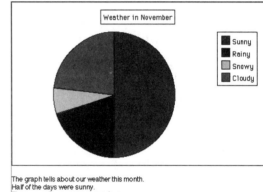

Step 6: Finish and Print

Make any necessary changes before printing the document. If the graph should be accidentally deleted, immediately select **Undo** from the **Edit** menu and the graph will reappear. **File...Print** the document. If desired, have students track the weather for one or two additional months during the school year. After creating pie graphs of those months, compare the weather information gathered.

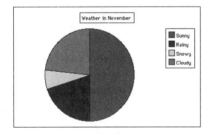

November

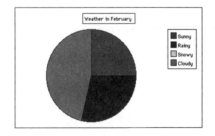

February

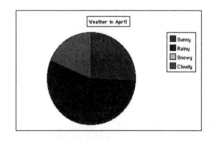

April

Activity 3: Weather Pie Graph and Reflection *(cont.)*

Weather for the Month of _____

Sunny Days	**Rainy Days**
Cloudy Days	**Snowy Days**

Tally Totals:

Sunny Days_____   **Rainy Days**_____   **Cloudy Days**_____   **Snowy Days**_____

Paint Programs: An Introduction

Young children are filled with creative thoughts and ideas. Bringing out this natural creativity is exciting through the use of computer paint programs.

One invaluable program is *Kid Pix 2*. A person with general computer skills can easily use this program, even without using the User's Guide or *Kid Pix 2* Basics instructions. Part of what makes *Kid Pix 2* so much fun is the element of discovery. There are so many tools and sounds to explore. Projects can be made with ease and the creation process is delightfully entertaining.

Kid Pix 2 not only gives students the opportunity to draw and paint pictures, but also provides tools for adding stamps and creating slide shows. If your school does not have *Kid Pix 2*, activities in this section can still be completed with similar programs such as *HyperStudio* or even the painting documents of some word processing programs like *ClarisWorks*. Due to the unique tools available in *Kid Pix 2*, other programs may be limited by comparison, but if properly modified, similar projects can be created. If your school does have *Kid Pix 2*, take some time to explore the program on your own and by reading *Kid Pix 2* Basics.

Kid Pix 2 Basics

This is a brief guide through the features of *Kid Pix 2*. More detailed instructions are available for creating projects, using menus and tools, and other tasks in the *Kid Pix 2* User's Guide that accompanies your software.

Getting Started

To begin, click to open *Kid Pix 2*. A drawing screen will appear with a menu bar across the top, a tool bar on the left side, and an options bar below.

Menus

The **File** menu gives you the opportunity to open New documents, Open existing documents, and Close documents. This menu also allows you to Save, Save As, Print, and Quit.

The **Edit** menu allows you to Undo unwanted actions. It also allows you to Cut, Copy, Paste, and Clear sections of a document.

The **Goodies** menu has many selections. The Small Kids Mode lets you "protect" your computer programs by keeping young children from straying out of *Kid Pix 2*. The Goodies menu also allows you to Edit Stamps, add letters and symbols to the wacky brush alphabet line with Alphabet Text, and Type Text. Additional selections in this menu include Tool Sounds, Record Sound, and Play Sound.

Paint Programs: An Introduction *(cont.)*

Kid Pix 2 Basics *(cont.)*

The **Switcheroo** menu gives you the opportunity to Swap Stamps and Swap Hidden Pictures. This menu also has features to explore such as DrawMe, ColorMe, and Wacky TV. In this menu, you may also Switch To SlideShow.

Tool Bar

The tool definitions below are listed in the order in which they appear on the tool bar.

The **Wacky Pencil** allows you to draw free-form lines.

The **Line** tool allows you to draw straight lines.

The **Rectangle** tool creates squares and rectangles in various sizes.

The **Oval** tool creates ovals in various sizes.

The **Wacky Brush** allows you to paint in a variety of ways.

The **Electric Mixer** changes your drawing in many silly ways.

The **Paint Can** fills a shape with a selected color or pattern.

The **Eraser** allows you to erase part of your picture in the standard way or in some interesting ways.

The **Text** tool is used to place letters, numbers, and symbols on the page.

The **Rubber Stamp** tool "stamps" pictures on the screen.

The **Moving Van** tool moves a portion of your picture from one place to another.

The **Undo Guy** immediately removes the last action performed on the screen. This is a very helpful tool!

The **Color Palette** allows you to select colors for drawing, painting, and text.

Paint Programs: An Introduction *(cont.)*

Kid Pix 2 Basics *(cont.)*

Options Bars

Each tool has at least one, if not several, options bars which appear below the drawing screen. Simply click on a tool in the tool bar and then click on a selection in the options bar. To access more options, click on the arrow at the right end of the bar.

How to Create a Slide Show

Follow the steps below to create a slide show of pictures created in *Kid Pix 2*.

1. Open **Slide Show** from the main menu of *Kid Pix 2*. A page of trucks will appear on the screen.

2. Click the small icon of the slide at the base of the first truck. This will bring up a small screen asking which picture you want as the first slide in the slide show.

3. Navigate to and double click on the desired picture. A thumbnail version of the picture will appear on the truck.

4. On the remaining trucks (or as many as you choose to use), continue selecting pictures in the same manner for the slide show.

5. Add sounds to each of the pictures by clicking on the music note on each truck. A menu of sounds will appear. You may preview the sounds before selecting the one you want. If a voice recording was already made and saved to accompany the picture, the music note icon will be in color (green). This indicates that the previously recorded sound has been added to the slide show automatically. If you choose to remove the recording and add another sound to accompany the picture, follow the directions given above.

Paint Programs: An Introduction *(cont.)*

Kid Pix 2 **Basics** *(cont.)*

6. Add transitions between the pictures in your slide show by clicking on the transition box. A menu of transitions will appear. You may preview the transitions before selecting the one you want.

7. Play the slide show by clicking on the arrow button at the bottom of the slide show screen.

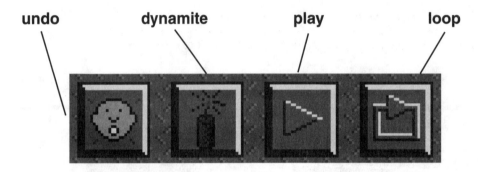

    undo   **dynamite**   **play**   **loop**

8. Loop the slides together to be played over and over by clicking on the loop button at the bottom of the slide show screen. To end the slide show, simply double click the mouse or press the **Command** and **Period** keys simultaneously on the keyboard.

9. Notice the Undo Guy at the bottom of the screen. Any operation can be removed by clicking this button immediately after the mistake is made.

10. Also notice the stick of dynamite at the bottom of the screen. If, at anytime during production, you are dissatisfied with the slide show you have created, simply click on this button to erase the show. This will not erase the original pictures, just their usage in the slide show.

11. **File...Save** the slide show. This is a great project to show parents at Open House or conferences.

Tip: Try this slide show idea for Open House. Create one big slide show of all students' *Kid Pix 2* creations and click to loop them together. This impressive show will continue to run throughout Open House for parents to view.

Help!

A brief Help document for *Kid Pix 2* is available in the apple menu. For additional help, see the *Kid Pix 2* User's Guide.

Activity 4: Fall Turns to Winter Picture

Teacher Note: This project has been created using *Kid Pix 2*. A similar project can be created using another drawing and painting program, if properly modified.

Students discuss the changing of the seasons and create a picture that shows Fall becoming Winter.

Background Knowledge: signs of the seasons in nature, cyclic order of seasons

Step 1: Discussion

Review the four seasons and their cyclic patterns in nature. Generate discussion among students about the signs in nature of Fall such as colored leaves, cool air, windy days, and falling leaves. List their ideas on chart paper for future reference.

Step 2: Create a Fall Picture Using *KidPix 2*

Follow these procedures to create a Fall picture.

1. Using the **File** menu, drag to **New** to open a new document.

2. Select the pencil from the tool bar; then click on the desired color to use. From the options bar below the screen, choose the line thickness and drawing pattern for the pencil. (You may want to experiment with different patterns and thicknesses before drawing the actual picture. To clear the screen after experimenting, simply click on the dynamite button on the tool bar and then click anywhere on the picture.) Draw a Fall picture showing items such as trees with colored leaves, leaves falling to the ground, cloudy skies, etc., following the steps in "*Kid Pix 2* Basics."

line thicknesses   **line patterns**

Activity 4: Fall Turns to Winter Picture *(cont.)*

Step 3: Add Snow to the Fall Picture

Your students will enjoy watching their pictures "snow" in this portion of the project.

1. Click on the mixer in the tool bar on the left side of the document.

2. Then, using the options bar that appears at the bottom of the page, select the box with the snowflake and raindrop on the right side of the bar.

snow option

3. Next, place the cursor on the picture and click. This will cause snowflakes to appear. Continued clicking on the picture creates additional snowflakes.

Step 4: Add Text

Complete the picture by adding text.

1. Open the **Goodies** menu at the top of the screen and drag to **Type Text**.

2. Decide where to begin the sentence and click on the screen in that location. Type a sentence about the picture. If more than one line is needed for the sentence, it is necessary to press the **Return** key on the keyboard. Unlike a typical word processing document, the text will not automatically shift to the next line. If you should happen to type beyond the screen, simply press the **Delete** key on the keyboard until the cursor can be seen again; then press the **Return** key to move to the next line and continue typing.

Step 5: Save and Print

Using the **File** menu, **Save** and **Print** the document.

Activity 5: Talking Weather Days Pictures

Teacher Note: This project has been created using *Kid Pix 2*. A similar project can be created using another drawing and painting program, if properly modified.

Students create pictures of days with different weather conditions using *Kid Pix 2* stamps and drawing. These colorful pictures are complete with text and sound.

Background Knowledge: attributes of various kinds of weather conditions

Step 1: Discussion of Weather Days

Ask students to name different kinds of weather and list each on the chalkboard or chart paper. For each type of weather, list students' responses for characteristics of that kind of day. Also, encourage your children to discuss the kinds of activities that can be done in different types of weather.

F E B R U A R Y						
Sun	**Mon**	**Tues**	**Weds**	**Thurs**	**Fri**	**Sat**
	1	2	3	4	5	6
7	8	9	10	11	12	13
14	15	16	17	18	19	20
21	22	23	24	25	26	27
28						

Step 2: Draw the Background for the Picture

Choose a type of weather to draw in your picture; then follow the steps below to create a background.

1. Select **File...New** to open a new document in *Kid Pix 2*.

2. From the tool bar, select the pencil and the desired color to begin the picture. Then select a line thickness from the options bar at the bottom of the screen.

line thicknesses   **line patterns**

3. Draw a simple background such as grass, sky, and a small body of water.

Activity 5: Talking Weather Days Pictures *(cont.)*

Draw the Background for the Picture *(cont.)*

4. To fill in an area with one color, draw the outline of the area to be colored, making sure to connect the ends of the outer line. Then select the paint can from the tool bar and click inside the area to be filled.

If any openings exist in the outer line, the entire screen will turn one color in this process. In this case, simply click on the **Undo Guy** from the tool bar and the previous screen will return. Then use the pencil tool to connect any existing line openings.

Step 3: Using Stamps to Create a Picture

Kid Pix 2 has three sets of stamps that can be used in your picture.

1. Select the stamp from the tool bar.

2. A series of stamps will appear in the options bar. By clicking on the arrow at the right end of the options bar, more stamps will appear. The Original *Kid Pix 2* stamp collection includes several appropriate choices for weather pictures, including a sun, a tree, flowers, an umbrella, and a lightning bolt.

3. Select the desired stamp and click on the screen where the stamp is to be placed. Make other selections by clicking on the desired stamps and then clicking on the screen.

Activity 5: Talking Weather Days Pictures *(cont.)*

Step 4: Access Other Stamp Collections

Follow the steps below to switch to other stamp collections in *Kid Pix 2*.

1. Select **Swap Stamps** from the **Switcheroo** menu at the top of the screen. Then select either City or Hodgepodge and click **OK**.

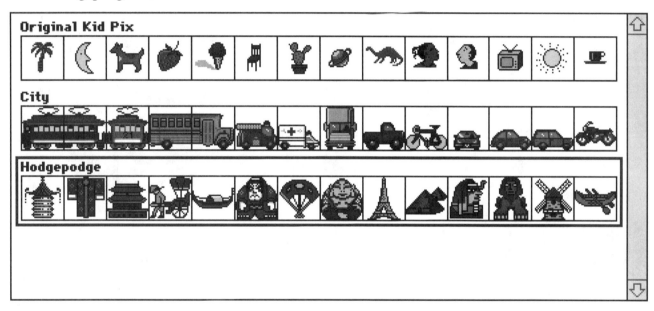

2. The City collection contains many stamps, including a variety of plants and trees. The Hodgepodge collection contains even more appropriate stamps, including leaves, clouds, birds, and snow-capped peaks.

3. Follow the same steps as described with the Original *Kid Pix 2* stamps to complete the picture.

Step 5: Add Text to the Picture

To add text to the picture, select **Type Text** from the **Goodies** menu. Click on the screen to place the cursor in the desired location. From the tool bar, select the desired text color. Then type a sentence to accompany the picture. If more than one line is needed for the sentence, it is necessary to press the **Return** key on the keyboard. Unlike a typical word processing document, the text will not automatically shift to the next line. If you should happen to type beyond the screen, simply press the **Delete** key on the keyboard until the cursor can be seen again; then press the **Return** key to move to the next line.

Activity 5: Talking Weather Days Pictures *(cont.)*

Step 6: Add Sound to the Picture

If your computer has a microphone, sound can be added to the picture. Select **Record Sound** from the **Goodies** menu. Click **Record** on the resulting window and read the sentence typed on the picture. Then click **Stop** and then **Save**. To play back the sound, click **Play** on the recording window or select **Play Sound** from the **Goodies** menu. (Each time the picture file is opened, the sound will play automatically.)

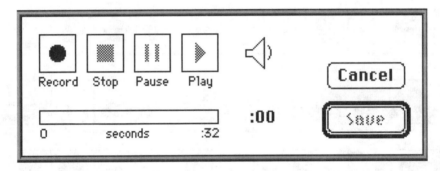

Step 7: Save and Print

Select **Save** and **Print** from the **File** menu. You may want to have students create a page for each kind of weather and then assemble the pages into a weather booklet. You can also create an on-screen slide show of the weather pages by following the steps on pages 21 and 22.

Activity 6: A Book of Clouds

Teacher Note: This project has been created using *Kid Pix 2*. A similar project can be created using another drawing and painting program, if properly modified.

Students use their knowledge of the different kinds of clouds to create three cloud pictures to be made into booklets and/or slide shows using *Kid Pix 2*.

Background Knowledge: characteristics of different types of clouds

Step 1: Discussion of Cloud Types

Review the three main types of clouds with your students (cirrus, stratus, and cumulus). You may choose to read *The Cloud Book* by Tomie de Daola (see Bibliography, page 48) to increase students' knowledge of clouds and generate discussion. Definitions of cirrus, stratus, and cumulus clouds are listed below. (See Teacher Created Material's Thematic Unit: Weather, TCM 273, beginning on page 13 for more cloud activities.)

Cirrus clouds are high, white clouds that appear in patches or thin, hairlike bands.

Stratus clouds are low clouds that are usually gray. These clouds often produce rain or snow.

Cumulus clouds have clearly defined outlines. They are white, puffy, and look like large pieces of cauliflower.

Step 2: Draw the Background for the Picture

Begin the picture by making a simple background.

1. Choose the first type of cloud picture to draw. Then click **File...New** to open a new document in *Kid Pix 2*.

2. From the tool bar, select the paint can and the desired color to use for the sky such as light or dark blue.

3. Click on the screen and one color will fill the entire area.

Activity 6: A Book of Clouds *(cont.)*

Step 3: Create a Cloud Picture

Follow these procedures to draw your clouds.

1. Select the pencil and the color for the clouds, from the tool bar.

2. Then choose a line thickness from the options bar below the picture.

line thicknesses   **line patterns**

3. Next draw the clouds. When drawing cirrus and cumulus clouds, you may want to fill them in with one color. To do this, draw the outline of the area to be colored, making sure to connect the ends of the outer line. Then select the paint can from the tool bar and click inside the area to be filled. If any openings exist in the outer line, the entire screen will turn one color in this process. In this case, click on the **Undo Guy** from the tool bar and the previous screen will return. Then use the pencil tool to connect the line openings.

Undo Guy

Step 4: Label the Picture

Add text to the picture by using the letters options bar.

1. Select the letter A from the tool bar.

2. Then from the option bar below, click on the first letter to be used in the label.

3. Click on the screen in the desired location. Select the next letter from the option bar and continue in the same manner until the label is complete. By clicking the arrow at the right end of the options bar, more letter, number, and punctuation choices are revealed.

A B C D E F G H I J K L M N

Activity 6: A Book of Clouds (cont.)

Step 5: Save and Print

Using the **File** menu, **Save** and **Print** the picture. Repeat the previous steps to create a picture for each type of cloud.

Big Book of Clouds

CUMULUS CLOUDS

Step 6: Create a Booklet and Slide Show

If desired, create a cover by making one additional picture with a title such as *A Book of Clouds*. Staple the pictures together to create a cloud booklet. Create a slide show from these pictures by following the steps in *Kid Pix 2* Slide Show on pages 21 and 22. Display the slide shows to parents at Open House, teacher-parent conferences, or in the school library for all to see (if a computer is available).

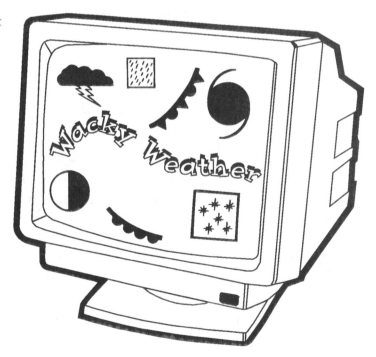

Desktop Publishing: An Introduction

Many times the need arises for more than just a word processing program. Desktop publishing offers the computer user alternative formats for items such as cards, banners, calendars, and signs with borders and other visuals.

Some very useful programs are *Print Shop Ensemble* for Macintosh, *Print Shop Ensemble III* for PC, or *Print Shop Deluxe III* for PC. All of these programs contain *Print Shop Deluxe* which is the basic program used to create the projects in this section of the book. Other desktop publishing programs include *Creative Writer* and *Student Writing Center.* A person with general word processing skills should have no trouble adjusting to desktop publishing programs, since these programs are very similar to word processing programs. The added benefit of desktop publishing is the ability to be more creative in making projects. For example, in the activity "Weather Fact Card," a card is produced combining a creative background, text, and graphics all in the same document.

Print Shop Deluxe in the Macintosh version, gives students the opportunity to create cards, banners, calendars, letterhead, and signs. These, combined with valuable information learned in class, make unique displays of students' knowledge. If your school does not have *Print Shop Deluxe*, activities described in this book can still be completed with similar programs, such as *Creative Writer* or *Student Writing Center.* If your school does have *Print Shop Deluxe*, get acquainted with this program in "*Print Shop Deluxe* Basics." Then let your students get started on these great projects.

Print Shop Deluxe Basics

This is a brief guide through the features of *Print Shop Deluxe.* More detailed instructions are available for creating projects, using menus and tools, and many other tasks in the *Print Shop Deluxe* User's Manual that accompanies your software. Follow the instructions carefully to have a successful experience with this outstanding desktop-publishing program.

Getting Started

While the Macintosh and PC versions of *Print Shop Deluxe* are similar, there are a few differences. When creating the projects in this section, additional steps for PC users will appear in parentheses.

When you click to open *Print Shop Deluxe*, the main screen will appear. This is where all of your projects will begin. Clicking on one of these buttons will get you started on your first project. (PC versions will bring up a window giving the choice to **Customize a Ready Made** project or **Start From Scratch.**)

Once you choose the type of project to create, the program will guide you through steps to choose a particular style for your project.

Desktop Publishing: An Introduction *(cont.)*

Print Shop Deluxe **Basics** *(cont.)*

Backdrops

Each time you create a project, you will be given the choice of backdrops. The screen (called a "dialog") that appears will show a list of **PSD** (*Print Shop Deluxe*) **Backdrops**.

If you choose not to have a backdrop, click the first choice on the list…**Blank Page**. Many more backdrop choices are available in different libraries (see "Changing Libraries" on page 34).

Layouts

After choosing a backdrop, you will be asked to choose a layout. Each type of *Print Shop Deluxe* project offers a variety of layouts. Review the following place-holder descriptions in order to understand the layouts.

Graphics Place Holders

 All of the graphics place holders have an icon of a bear face on them. There are three different kinds of graphics—square, row, and column. You will have a large selection of graphics choices for your project, depending on which type of graphics place holder you choose.

Borders and Mini-Borders

Borders and mini-borders do not have icons. They will appear in the layout as a blank place holder outlining your project.

Borders come in large and small widths that, for Macintosh, can be adjusted by clicking the **Size** menu on the dialog window and dragging to **Large** or **Small**. (PC users can go to the **Object** menu, select **Border Size**, and then select **Normal** or **Wide**.) Borders always surround the outer edges of the project and cannot be moved or stretched.

Mini-borders can be placed anywhere on the project and are often used to outline graphics or text blocks. These borders can be rotated, stretched, and size altered.

Desktop Publishing: An Introduction *(cont.)*

Print Shop Deluxe **Basics** *(cont.)*

Horizontal and Vertical Ruled Line Graphics

 A **ruled line** place holder has an icon that looks like three dashes. These graphics are often used to separate sections of a project or to add decorative flair.

Headlines and Text Blocks

 Headline place holders have an icon of an exclamation mark in them. They come in a variety of sizes and shapes (depending on the layout you choose) which can be adjusted as desired.

 Text place holders have a letter T icon and come in a variety of sizes.

Now you can choose a layout for your project. You may preview different layouts by clicking one time on a selection or you may choose **No Layout** which allows you to create your own unique layout (see "Using Tools" on page 36). When you have selected a layout, click **OK** and it will appear on the screen.

Choosing Graphics

To view the graphics available for each of the graphics place holders, double click the place holder and a dialog window, listing your choices, will appear.

Changing Libraries

There are many different libraries from which to choose. To access these libraries in Macintosh, double click on the graphic place holder and click on **Change Library**. Then open the **Libraries** folder and click to open the desired graphics library. Select a graphic; then click **OK** and it will appear on your project. (PC users double click on the place holder, go to the Graphic Library menu and select a library from the list.)

Desktop Publishing: An Introduction *(cont.)*

Print Shop Deluxe **Basics** *(cont.)*

Disc 2 Graphics

Print Shop Ensemble for Macintosh, *Print Shop Ensemble III* for PC, and *Print Shop Deluxe* III for PC all include a second graphics disk. To utilize this disk in Macintosh, follow these steps.

1. Insert Disc 2 into the CD-ROM drive.

2. After selecting a project, backdrop, and layout, double click on the graphics place holder.

3. Click to **Change Libraries**.

4. From the resulting dialog window, click on *Print Shop Deluxe* and drag to **Desktop**.

5. From the desktop menu, drag to **Disc 2**. A list of graphics libraries will appear in the window.

6. Choose the desired library from the list and then proceed in the manner explained above to add a graphics choice to your project.

   (PC users, simply insert Disc 2 into the CD-ROM drive. After a brief pause, the new graphics libraries will be available in the Graphic Libraries menu.)

Adding Headlines and Text

Double click on the headline place holder and a dialog window will appear. In this window you will type the headline. You will also have font, style, and headline shape options. When the headline is complete, click **OK** and it will appear on your project.

Desktop Publishing: An Introduction *(cont.)*

Print Shop Deluxe Basics *(cont.)*

To type the text on your project, double click on the text place holder and a cursor will appear in the text block. (In PC versions, an **Edit Text** window will appear. When finished typing, click **OK**.) After typing, you may highlight the text and change the **Size, Font,** and **Style** by using the **Text** menu. Click outside the text block to end typing. At this point, you may move the text block anywhere on the project by clicking on the text again (revealing a small, dark square in each corner), and dragging it to the desired location.

Using Tools

You may choose to design your own project layout. This can be done easily by using *Print Shop Deluxe* tools. (In the PC versions of *Print Shop Deluxe*, the tools are visible in a single row at the top of the screen, rather than in a tool palette as shown.) The tools are briefly described below.

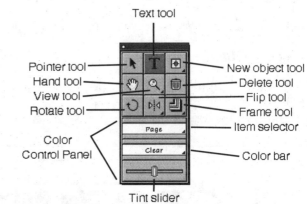

Pointer tool—allows you to select, resize, and move objects.

Text tool—lets you add text blocks.

Object tool—allows you to add graphics, text, or headlines.

Hand tool—allows you to move your entire project on the screen.

View tool—lets you view your project in a variety of ways.

Delete tool—allows you to delete an object.

Rotate tool—lets you turn an object on the screen.

Flip tool—allows you to flip graphics.

Frame tool—allows you to add a frame to your project.

Item selector—lets you add color to selected objects.

Color bar—gives a variety of color choices.

Tint slider—lets you change the shade of colored objects.

Help!

In Macintosh, there are two ways to get help within *Print Shop Deluxe*. You may select the **Help** button when it is available in a dialog window or go to the **Apple** menu and drag to **Help**. (In PC versions, **Help** buttons are available in the dialog windows.)

Activity 7: Weather in the United States

Teacher Note: This project has been created using *Print Shop Deluxe*. Similar projects can be created using other desktop publishing programs, if properly modified. (Additional instructions for PC users will appear in parentheses.)

Students make a sign with a weather-map graphic and write about United States weather conditions using *Print Shop Deluxe*.

Background Knowledge: types of weather

Step 1: Weather Discussion

After discussing the weather in your area, encourage students to discuss weather conditions in other parts of the country. Help students understand that certain parts of the country are typically warmer, cooler, rainier, or snowier than others. Have students tell about the weather in parts of the country they have visited.

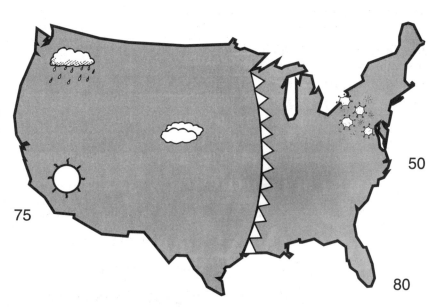

Provide several copies of national weather maps from your local newspaper. (You may want to enlarge the weather map to display for the whole group.) Have students identify the map key and locate various types of weather indicated on the map.

Step 2: Create the Sign Graphics

Use the following steps to create a weather-map graphic on the sign.

1. From the main menu of *Print Shop Deluxe*, select **Sign**. (PC users select **Signs & Posters**. From the next window, select **Start From Scratch**.) Then click on **Tall**.

2. A list of Portrait Backdrops will appear. From this list, select **Blank Page** and then click **OK**.

3. A list of Portrait Layouts will appear. From this list, select **Sign 12** and click **OK**.

4. The layout of the sign will appear on the screen. Double click on the graphic place holder at the top of the sign.

Activity 7: Weather in the United States *(cont.)*

Create the Sign Graphics *(cont.)*

5. A menu for Square Graphics will appear. Macintosh users click on **Change Library** at the bottom of the menu. Then click to open the **Libraries** folder (if it is not already open). Scroll down to **PSD Nature** and open the file.

   (PC users click on **Graphic Library** and select **Nature** library.)

6. Select **Weather Map** from the library and click **OK**. The weather map will now appear on the sign.

Step 3: Create the Sign Headline

Use the following steps to create a headline.

1. Double click on the headline place holder.

2. Type a headline such as *United States Weather* and click **OK**. The headline will appear on your project.

Step 4: Add the Sign Text

Add text by using the following procedures.

1. Double click on the text place holder and a cursor will appear on the screen. (PC users will see an **Edit Text** window.)

2. Based on the information gained from the national weather map, type sentences telling about weather conditions in several different parts of the country.

3. Then click on the pointer tool in the tool palette. This will set the text into the project and prepare for rearranging text and graphics positioning. (For PC, just click **OK** to set the text in place on the screen.)

Activity 7: Weather in the United States *(cont.)*

Step 5: Rearrange Graphic and Text

If desired, reduce and move the text box to the lower portion of the sign. To reduce the size of the box, click and drag on the dark square in the lower right corner. To move the box, click in the center of the box and drag to the desired location. The same can be done with the headline and the graphic.

Weather in the United States

Today is Monday, Nov. 3, 1997.
It is snowing in New York.
It is raining in North Carolina.
It is windy in Texas.
It is sunny in Arizona.

Step 6: Save and Print

Save and **Print** a copy of the completed sign using the **File** menu at the top of the screen. If desired, have each student track the weather in a different state for several days and write about it in the project. Then attach the completed project to a large outline of the featured state cut from black construction paper.

Activity 8: A Week of Weather

Teacher Note: This project can be created using *Print Shop Deluxe*. Another desktop publishing program could be used to create a similar project, if properly modified. (Additional instructions for PC users will appear in parentheses.)

Students keep track of the weather for one week and then record the information on a weekly calendar, complete with graphics and text. (Use this project in addition to the activity in Teacher Created Materials' Thematic Unit: *Weather*, TCM 273, on pages 49 and 50.)

Background Knowledge: identifying signs of weather

Step 1: Tracking the Weather

Explain to students that they will keep track of the weather for one week. This can be done individually or as a class. An empty calendar page can be provided to students for tracking the weather for the week.

Step 2: Create the Calendar and Graphics

Make the basic calendar by performing these simple tasks.

1. Select **Calendar** from the main menu of *Print Shop Deluxe*. (PC users will select **Start From Scratch** from the next window.)

2. Click on **Weekly.** Macintosh users then select **Tall**. (PC users will be asked to select the calendar orientation later.)

3. A dialog window will ask you to choose the month, date, and year for the calendar. Do this and click **OK**. (PC users will now see a **Calendar Orientation** screen. From this window, select **Tall**.)

Activity 8: A Week of Weather *(cont.)*

Create the Calendar and Graphics *(cont.)*

4. A screen of Portrait Backdrops will appear. Select **Blank Page** from the list and click **OK**.

5. The Portraits Layout menu will appear. Select **Calendar 1** from the list and click **OK**.

6. The layout of the calendar will appear on the screen. Click on the Object tool on the tool palette or tool bar and drag to **Square Graphic**. Double click the graphic place holder on the screen.

7. The square graphics dialog window will appear on the screen. Macintosh users click on the **Change Library** button. Follow the instructions in *Print Shop Deluxe* Basics on pages 34 and 35 for utilizing Disc 2 Graphics. (PC users insert Disc 2 into the CD- ROM drive, go to the Graphic Shapes menu and select Square Graphics, and the new libraries will be available in the Graphic Libraries menu.)

8. When you have opened Disc 2, scroll down to **Plants and Flowers**.

9. There are weather graphics in this library that can be used to show the weather for each day on the calendar such as a variety of suns, sun and clouds, snowflakes, snowmen, rain scenes, and umbrellas.

10. Select the desired graphic for Monday and click **OK**.

11. Adjust the size of the graphic by clicking and dragging on the dark square in its lower right corner. Move it beside the word Monday by clicking and dragging the graphic.

12. Repeat this process for each day of the week.

Step 3: Add Final Graphic

If desired, place a decorative weather graphic in the graphics place holder below the calendar. The graphic shown in this project is the **Weather Vane** from the **Plants and Flowers** menu on Disc 2. This graphic can be moved to the top of the calendar as shown on page 42. If you should choose not to use an additional graphic, click on the place holder to highlight it and then press the **Delete** key on the keyboard to remove it.

Activity 8: A Week of Weather *(cont.)*

Step 4: Add Text to the Calendar

Use a text box on each day of the calendar to tell about that day's weather.

1. For each of the days on the calendar, click on the Object tool in the tool palette and drag to **Text block** (PC users select **Text**).

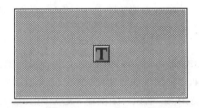

2. Use the same process as with the graphics above to adjust the size and location of the text block.

3. Double click on the text place holder and type a sentence or two telling about the weather each day. (PC users will see an **Edit Text** window. When finished typing, click **OK**.)

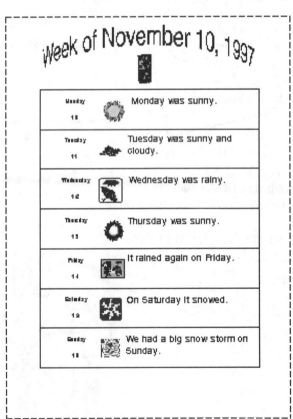

Step 5: Save and Print

Go to the **File** menu to **Save** and **Print** the calendar. Display the completed projects on a bulletin board entitled, "We're Weather Watchers."

Activity 9: Weather Fact Card

Teacher Note: This project has been created using *Print Shop Deluxe*. Another desktop publishing program could be used to create a similar project. (Additional instructions for PC users will appear in parentheses.)

Students create greeting cards containing graphics and weather facts learned from the weather unit.

Background Knowledge: interesting facts about various kinds of weather

Step 1: Discover Interesting Weather Facts

Provide a variety of weather-related books for your students. Allow them to skim the books to discover interesting weather facts about the sun, rain, snow, wind, clouds, etc. Then have students gather in a group to share their facts with one another. Record the facts on chart paper for all to see. Explain to the children that they will each create a weather-fact card. Ask each child to choose one or two favorite facts from the chart to include in the card.

Step 2: Create the Card Cover

Make the cover of the card by following these instructions.

1. Select **Greeting Card** from the *Print Shop Deluxe* menu. (In PC, select **Start From Scratch** in the next window.)

2. Then click to choose the desired card style.

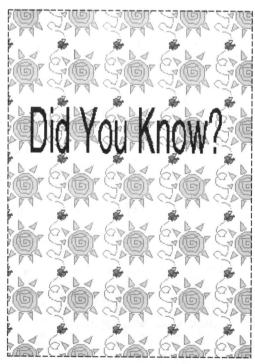

Activity 9: Weather Fact Card *(cont.)*

Create the Card Cover *(cont.)*

3. From the Portrait Backdrop menu, select a weather-related background. Listed below are several appropriate suggestions from *Print Shop Deluxe* libraries. Click **Change Library** and open the **Libraries** folder to access the various graphics.

> **PSD Backdrops:**
> Winter Snowscape
> Winter Child

> **Graphics Plus Backdrops (Mac only):**
> Winter Village

> **Sampler Backdrops:**
> Clouds
> Lacy Snowflake
> Sun and Butterfly

4. From the Portrait Layout menu, select **No Layout** and then click **OK**.

 5. Click the Object tool on the tool palette or tool bar and drag to **Headline**.

 6. Double click the headline place holder and type "Did You Know?" Then click **OK**.

Step 3: Create the Inside of the Card

Design the inside of the fact card using the procedures below.

1. Select **Inside of card** from the **Project** menu.

2. Choose a backdrop, if desired, otherwise choose **Blank Page**.

3. Select **No Layout** from the layout menu.

4. Click the Object tool on the tool palette or tool bar and drag to **Text Block.** (In PC, select **Text.**)

5. Adjust the size and location of the text block. Double click the text place holder; then type one or more weather facts. (PC users click **OK** when finished typing.)

6. Click the Object tool again and drag to either **Rows Graphic** or **Column Graphic**.

Activity 9: Weather Fact Card *(cont.)*

Create the Inside of the Card *(cont.)*

7. Double click on the graphic place holder. Then choose a graphic for the inside of the card and drag it to the desired location. The following is a list of weather/season-related row graphics.

PSD Rows: Snowman & Hearth	**Celebrations Rows:** (PC—All Libraries) Harvest	**Graphics Plus Rows 1** (Mac only): Spring Sunflies

The following is a list of weather/season-related column graphics.

PSD Columns: Lightning bolt	**PSD 2 Columns:** (PC—All Libraries) Desert Heat	**Sampler Columns:** Summer Winter

Step 4: Save, Print, and Fold the Card

Follow these directions and your project is complete.

Using the **File** menu, **Save** and **Print** the card. To fold the card, place the page on a flat surface with the print facedown. Then fold the top of the paper to meet the bottom of the paper and crease it. Then fold the card across so that the poem is on the inside. Have students take their cards home to display their weather knowledge to parents.

Exploring on the Internet

When considering instructional and research resources, try complementing your curriculum with information from Web sites on the Internet. The resources available to you on the Internet are virtually endless. One can find information, pictures, videos, and sound on nearly anything and every topic.

Logging On

If you are unfamiliar with the Internet, elicit help from a co-worker to log onto your school's network and Web browser. The network is the phone line access you use to get to the Internet. A Web browser is the "viewer" you use to see what's out there. Access to the Internet may be a two-step process. You may need to first log onto a local network before hooking into a Web browser like *Netscape* or *Mosaic*. Others, like *American Online* and *CompuServ* are networks and Web browsers all in one.

Finding Information

After you are logged onto a Web browser, you may begin searching for related topics and specific information. *Excite, Yahoo, Infoseek, Lycos,* and *Magellan* are popular search bases. By typing in a specific http://www.? (or uniform resource locator), you should be able to locate any Web site from any search base. You can also type in a subject of interest in the "search" box and click on **Search** to retrieve a host of related Web sites you may consider visiting.

Have fun investigating the many Web sites available to you on the Internet. When you find a site that looks interesting, you can bookmark it by clicking the **Bookmark** prompt from the task bar at the top. Then, when you visit this Web site again, you need only find your bookmark from the list and click on it. The computer will take you right to that page.

Cool Web Sites

The Web sites listed here can be found by using any Internet service provider (e.g., *America Online, CompuServ, Prodigy)* or using a direct Internet access called Point to Point Protocol (PPP) through your school or a variety of services (e.g., *Earthlink, FlashNet,* etc.). Then you can view the Internet through Netscape and search in *Yahoo*. Regardless of the network and Web browser your school uses, you should be able to search the database for the Web sites listed in this guide.

Keep in mind that Web sites tend to change over time. If these Web sites are no longer in existence, you can still find information by typing in a specific topic to search, such as "weather."

Exploring on the Internet *(cont.)*

Cool Web Sites *(cont.)*

The Weather Dude
http://nwlink.com/~wxdude/

This teacher—and kid—friendly site is hosted by a weather forecaster. You'll find facts, songs to download, activities, teacher and parent information, and links to other sites such as *The Weather Channel's* Weather Classroom.

The Weather Unit
http://faldo.atmos.uius.edu/WEATHER/weather.html

This teacher-friendly site provides a comprehensive weather unit with activities for math, reading and writing, drama, social studies, music, art, and much more.

Earth Watch Weather on Demand
http://earthwatch.com/

Use this site to find 3D weather information and forecasts. There are also Earth Watch links to Stormwatch, satellite and radar information, weather headlines, and more.

National Weather Service
http://205.156.54.206/

This site is a great resource with information about current weather, climate data, and a variety of other weather resources.

The Weather Underground: K-12 Weather Curriculum
http://groundhog.sprl.umich.edu/curriculum

This site provides teachers with information and student activities about hurricanes, forecasting, stormwatch, and much, much more.

Dan's Wild Wild Weather Page
http://www.whnt19.com/kidwx/

Hosted by a meteorologist, this site features information about a variety of weather topics such as El Nino, clouds, temperature, lightning, and many others.

About Rainbows
www.bonus.com/bonus/card/aboutrainbows.html

This site provides information about what rainbows are, how double rainbows are formed, what makes the colors of a rainbow, etc.

The Tornado Project Online
http://www.bonus.com/bonus/card/tornadoonline.html

Complete with photos, stories, books, myths, and FAQs, this tornado site is sure to interest students.

Resources and Bibliography

Software

ClarisWorks **4.0.** (1995). Claris Corporation.

Creative Writer. (1994). Microsoft Corporation.

HyperStudio. (1996). Roger Wagner Publishing, Inc.

Kid Pix 2. (1994). Broderbund Software, Inc.

Magic School Bus CD-ROM series. (1996). Microsoft Corporation.

Print Shop Ensemble (for Macintosh). (1992 1996). Broderbund Software, Inc.

Print Shop Ensemble III (for PC). (1992 1996). Broderbund Software, Inc.

Print Shop Deluxe III (for PC). (1992 1996). Broderbund Software, Inc.

Student Writing Center. (1986-1993). The Learning Company and Fore Front Corporation.

Literature

de Paola, Tomie. *The Cloud Book.* Holiday House, 1975.

Teacher Created Materials Resources

TCM 273 *Weather Thematic Unit*

TCM 611 *Hands On Minds On Science: Weather*

TCM 798 *Winter Activities*

TCM 809 *Autumn Activities*

TCM 1000 *Weather Learning Center Display Board*

TCM 1156 *Geosafari Cards: Weather*

TCM 2089 *The Magic School Bus: Inside A Hurricane*

TCM 2182 *Kid Pix for Terrified Teachers*

TCM 2185 *ClarisWorks for Terrified Teachers*

Online Services

America Online (800) 827-6364

Compuserv (800)848-8990

Netscape (800) 254-1900

Prodigy (800) 776-3449 ext. 629

Net Search Providers

Excite, Yahoo, Infoseek, Lycos, Magellan